THE
TOTALLY
TEATIME
COOKBOOK

D0037490

Copyright © 1995 by Helene Siegel and Karen Gillingham.
Illustrations © 1995 by Carolyn Vibbert. All rights reserved.
No part of this book may be reproduced or transmitted in any
form or by any means, electronic or mechanical, including
photocopying, recording, or by any information or storage and
retrieval system, without the express permission of the publisher.

The Totally Teatime Cookbook is produced by becker&mayer!, Ltd.

Cover illustration and design: Dick Witt

Interior typesetting and design: Susan Hernday

Interior illustrations: Carolyn Vibbert

Library of Congress Cataloging-in-Publication Data:

Siegel, Helene.
    Totally Teatime Cookbook / by Helene Siegel and Karen Gillingham.
        p. cm.
    ISBN 0-89087-755-6
    1. Cookery (Teatime)   I. Gillingham, Karen.   II. Title.
    TX819.C6S53 1995
    641.6'373—dc20   95-10967
                          CIP
                    Celestial Arts Publishing
                         P.O. Box 7123
                       Berkeley, CA 94707

Other cookbooks in this series:
The Totally Garlic Cookbook
The Totally Chile Pepper Cookbook
The Totally Mushroom Cookbook
The Totally Corn Cookbook
The Totally Cookies Cookbook
The Totally Coffee Cookbook
The Totally Muffins Cookbook

THE
TOTALLY
TEATIME
COOKBOOK

By
Helene Siegel
and
Karen Gillingham

Illustrations by Carolyn Vibbert

CELESTIAL ARTS
BERKELEY, CALIFORNIA

I'm a little tea pot
Short and stout
Here is my handle
Here is my spout
When I get all steamed up hear me shout
Just tip me over and pour me out.

Ever since a group of rowdy revolutionaries dressed up like Mohawk Indians and tossed 340 chests of good British tea into Boston Harbor, we Americans have had tangled emotions regarding tea.

We may drink it when we are sick or when we are out of coffee, but deep down in our collective food memories we just don't trust it—unless it is poured over a large glass of ice and flavored with fruit.

Now, since one of the best things about being American cooks is our ability to borrow foods from the world's great cuisines and then modify them to suit our needs and fashions, we think it is high time Americans reconsidered tea—and in particular, the foods that accompany it.

We are not advocating a return to white gloves and proper etiquette here. What we suggest is inviting some friends over late on a weekend morning or afternoon for homemade ginger scones or biscuits, fresh apple cake, smoked turkey sandwiches, and a selection of cookies. Then sit back and give the Brits some credit for knowing how to entertain with ease, style, and panache.

You don't even have to serve tea to enjoy these hand-held tidbits and mood enhancers—though it does add an air of authenticity. Lemonade, sparkling water, or champagne will do just fine. As for coffee, it won't do any harm to have a pot available for any caffeine-crazed patriots in the room.

CUCUMBER AND DAIKON SPROUTS SANDWICH

Sliced paper thin and delicately layered between the leaves of a sandwich, cucumbers take on a meaning only the British can fathom. The best tasting cucumbers are the small, thin-skinned pickling cukes.

pickling cucumbers, peeled and
very thinly sliced lengthwise
rice wine vinegar
thinly sliced wheat bread
softened butter
salt and pepper
daikon sprouts, ends trimmed

Place cucumber slices on plate, lightly drizzle with vinegar and let sit 15 minutes.

Spread each slice of bread thinly with butter.

Arrange cucumbers in single layer over half bread slices. Season with salt and pepper. Top with thin layer of sprouts and slice of buttered bread. Press to seal. Trim crusts and slice into fingers or triangles.

Tea Sandwich Tips

The point of the tea sandwich is not to fill you up, but to leave room for more—an un-American idea at best. To achieve daintier sandwiches: purchase very thinly sliced bread and freeze an hour or two before handling; keep fillings at room temperature for easier spreading, spread first (all the way out to the edges), then trim and discard crusts; use a serrated blade for neat trimming and cutting.

TOMATO, WATERCRESS, AND CHIVE BUTTER SANDWICH

These slender sandwiches really highlight the sweet, tart flavor of tomato.

4 tablespoons butter, softened
juice of ½ lemon
½ bunch fresh chives, sliced
12 slices thinly sliced white or wheat bread
tomato, very thinly sliced
salt and pepper
watercress, stems trimmed, washed and dried

Mix together butter, lemon juice, and chives in small bowl to make a paste. Spread thinly over all the bread. Arrange one layer of tomatoes over half

the bread slices and season with salt and pepper.
Top with 2 or 3 watercress leaves and top with slice
of buttered bread. Press to seal, trim crusts and cut
into fingers or triangles.

MAKES 12 SMALL SANDWICHES

Tea in England

Like the rest of Europe, England was a coffee drinking
nation when tea was introduced by Catherine Bragança of
Portugal upon marrying Charles II in the middle of the 17th
century. Green tea soon became the rage at court, but the
rest of the population remained devoted to ale for breakfast.

It took the tea gardens of the mid-18th century to truly
popularize the drink. In these elaborately decorated public
spaces, men and women gathered to dine, dance, display the
latest fashions, and sip tea—giving tea the social cachet it
needed to make the jump from hot beverage to cultural icon.

SMOKED TURKEY TOMATO SANDWICH

*If tomato preserves are not available, very finely julienned
roasted red pepper strips are also delicious.*

1¼ pounds whole skinless, boneless
   smoked turkey breast
4 tablespoons butter, softened
freshly ground black pepper
Tabasco sauce
tomato preserves
thinly sliced egg or white bread

Cut turkey breast in large dice. Purée in food
processor till smooth. Cut butter into tablespoon-
sized pieces and add to turkey. Purée. Season to
taste with pepper and Tabasco. Spread half the
bread slices with turkey paste and half with tomato
preserves. Close, trim crusts, and cut into triangles.

MAKES 1½ CUPS SPREAD

FARMER'S SPREAD SANDWICH

Farmer's cheese is a mild white cheese similar to dry cottage cheese. It is available in packages at the supermarket.

1 (7.5-ounce) package farmer's cheese
2 tablespoons heavy cream
4 radishes, trimmed and finely diced
2 scallions, white part only, finely chopped
2 teaspoons fresh chopped Italian parsley
freshly ground black pepper
thinly sliced wheat or black bread

In small bowl, combine cheese and cream by hand. Add the vegetables, parsley, and pepper and mix lightly. Spread on half of bread and top with uncoated slice. Trim crusts and cut into triangles.

MAKES ABOUT 16 SMALL SANDWICHES

CURRIED EGG SANDWICHES

*Along with tea, the British brought back from India a
taste for curries to heat up a rather bland palate.*

6 eggs, hard boiled
⅓ cup mayonnaise
2 tablespoons chopped mango chutney
   (optional)
¾ teaspoon curry powder
salt and pepper
thinly sliced white bread

Peel eggs and coarsely chop. Combine eggs,
mayonnaise, chutney, and curry powder in bowl.
Mix with fork, mashing eggs in process. Season to
taste with salt and pepper. Spread one slice of bread
with egg mixture. Top with second slice, trim crusts,
and cut. Cut in half diagonally and trim crusts.

MAKES 8

CHOCOLATE TEA SANDWICHES

Why couldn't we all grow up in England, where parents have the decency to serve little children afternoon snacks of sugar and chocolate sandwiches?

12 slices thinly sliced white or egg bread
1 (3-ounce) package cream cheese, at room
    temperature
¼ cup brown sugar
¼ cup grated semisweet chocolate

Spread 6 slices bread with cream cheese. Sprinkle with brown sugar, then chocolate. Top each with second slice of bread. Cut each sandwich into halves, thirds, or shapes using cookie cutters. Trim and discard crusts.

MAKES 6

SHRIMP SALAD SANDWICHES

As young girls, we thought shrimp salad sandwiches smacked of big city sophistication. They still taste delicious.

³/₄ pound cooked bay shrimp
2 tablespoons mayonnaise
1 tablespoon lemon juice
3 or 4 dashes Tabasco
freshly ground black pepper
1 celery stalk, trimmed and finely diced
thinly sliced egg bread or miniature rolls

Process ½ pound of the shrimp in a food processor until finely chopped. Add mayonnaise, lemon juice, Tabasco, and pepper. Pulse into spread. Roughly chop remaining ¼ pound shrimp and add with celery, to spread. Stir to combine. Spread on bread, trim crusts.

MAKES ABOUT 1 CUP

The Plant

All true tea is derived from the *Camellia sinensis plant, an evergreen shrub indigenous to an area up to 42 degrees north of the equator. The best tea is grown on plantations in China, Taiwan, Sri Lanka, India, and Japan. Since only the top two leaves and a final bud is used for tea making, first rate tea is still hand picked—mostly by women. Machine picking results in damaged leaves and a less distinctive brew reserved for lesser quality tea bags.*

The taste of tea is determined by how it is processed, the size of the leaf, and blending. There are three general categories: black, green, and Oolong. Black tea is fermented, green is unfermented, and Oolong is partially fermented. Hearty black teas from India and Sri Lanka are most popular in the U.K., Europe, and the U.S.; more herbaceous green teas are the rule in Japan, and delicate Oolongs are popular in China.

SALLY LUNN
WELSH RABBIT

Welsh Rabbit, or Rarebit, is essentially a spiced grilled cheese sandwich served open-faced. As for the name itself, there are unsubstantiated reports of a Welshman who returned home empty-handed from a hunting expedition—hence the grilled cheese sandwich for dinner concept.

3 eggs
1 teaspoon mustard
¼ teaspoon salt
⅛ teaspoon white pepper
2 tablespoons Worcestershire sauce
¾ pound sharp Cheddar cheese, diced
2 Sally Lunn Buns (page 34) or 4 English
    muffins, split and toasted

Preheat broiler.

Combine eggs with mustard, salt, pepper, and Worcestershire sauce in food processor. Process until blended. Add cheese and process to form thick paste. Spread mixture over cut surfaces of buns or muffins. Place on baking sheet under broiler until melted and beginning to brown. Serve hot.

SERVES 4

Measuring the Leaves

Since larger leaves produce a more distinctive flavor they are the most prized. Black and Oolong teas are sorted according to size: Orange pekoe are the largest; broken orange pekoe are smaller or broken leaves; fannings are the smallest leaf fragments; and dust is what it sounds like—reserved for tea bags. The term pekoe never refers to flavor, just leaf size.

SCONES
CRUMPETS
AND
TEA BREADS

IRISH SODA BREAD

Try half whole wheat flour for a fuller, nuttier flavor in this traditional craggy soda bread from Eileen Wohl and her grandmother, Mary Frances Regan Lynch. Serve plain, hot from the oven, or sliced and toasted the next day.

1 $\frac{2}{3}$ cups milk
$\frac{1}{2}$ stick butter, melted
1 egg, beaten
1 cup golden raisins
$\frac{1}{8}$ teaspoon vinegar
4 cups all-purpose flour
$\frac{1}{4}$ cup sugar
2 teaspoons baking powder
1 teaspoon baking soda
1 teaspoon salt
2 tablespoons caraway seed flour
   for dusting

Preheat oven to 375 degrees F. Grease a 9-inch round cake pan or cast iron skillet.

In large bowl, whisk together milk, butter, egg, raisins, and vinegar. In another bowl, combine remaining ingredients. Add dry mixture to liquid and stir until evenly moistened. Knead on floured board about 10 times.

Place dough in prepared pan and dust top with a handful of flour. Bake 50 minutes, until bread sounds hollow when tapped. Remove from pan and cool on rack.

MAKES 1 LARGE LOAF

WHEAT CURRANT SCONES

*Our appetite for these authentic buttermilk scones is
limited only by time and reason.*

1 ½ cups all-purpose flour
1 ½ cups whole wheat flour
1 tablespoon baking powder
1 teaspoon baking soda
¼ cup sugar
¼ teaspoon salt
1 stick butter, cold and cut in ¼-inch slices
1 cup currants or raisins
1 cup buttermilk
1 egg, beaten

Preheat oven to 450 degrees F.

In large bowl, combine flours, baking powder,
soda, sugar, and salt. Mix with fork. Add butter and

blend with fingertips or pastry blender until butter is evenly dispersed and mixture resembles coarse meal. Add currants or raisins and buttermilk and stir just until evenly moistened.

Turn out onto floured board and gently knead until shaggy, dry dough forms. Cut in half and pat each piece into a disk. Lightly roll each into 6-inch circle. Transfer to uncoated baking sheet and brush tops with beaten egg. Score each into 6 wedges. Bake 20 minutes, until tops are brown. Cool on racks and serve.

MAKES 12

GINGER BUTTERMILK SCONES

*Ginger adds so much pizzazz, these moist scones
need very little enhancement.*

3 cups all-purpose flour
1 tablespoon baking powder
1 teaspoon baking soda
2 tablespoons sugar
1 stick butter, cold and cut in ¼-inch slices
½ cup crystallized ginger, rinsed, dried, and
   finely chopped
1¼ cups buttermilk
2 tablespoons melted butter and raw brown
   sugar for glaze (optional)

Preheat oven to 425 degrees F.
In large mixing bowl, combine flour, baking

powder, soda, and sugar. Mix with fork. Add butter and blend with fingertips or pastry blender until mixture resembles coarse meal. Mix in ginger. Pour in buttermilk and stir to combine.

Turn out onto lightly floured board and gently knead to form smooth disk. Cut into three pieces. Pat each into a circle, flatten lightly with palm of hand and transfer to uncoated baking pan. Brush tops with melted butter and sprinkle with sugar as desired. Score each into quarters. Bake 25 minutes, until golden. Cool on racks, break apart and serve.

MAKES 12

CORN ROSEMARY SCONES

*A cross between a scone and a biscuit, these tender yellow
disks are delicious moistened with
a dab of cream or butter and a spoonful of jam.*

2 cups all-purpose flour
½ cup yellow cornmeal
2 teaspoons baking powder
2 tablespoons sugar
½ teaspoon salt
6 tablespoons butter, cold and cut in ¼-inch
    slices
2 teaspoons grated lemon zest
1 teaspoon fresh chopped rosemary
1 egg
¾ cups half-and-half
1 egg, beaten and confectioners' sugar for glaze

Preheat oven to 400 degrees F.

In large mixing bowl, combine flour, cornmeal, baking powder, sugar, and salt. Mix with fork. Add butter and blend with fingertips or pastry blender until butter is evenly mixed in chunks. Blend in lemon zest and rosemary.

Beat egg in small bowl with half-and-half. Pour into flour mixture and stir with wooden spoon. Turn out onto floured board and lightly knead. Lightly roll to form 12-inch circle. Using fluted or plain 3-inch cookie cutters, cut out dough. Transfer to uncoated baking sheet and brush tops with egg. Re-roll scraps and cut remaining dough. Bake 10 minutes, remove from oven, generously sift confectioners' sugar over tops and bake 5 minutes longer. Set aside to cool on racks.

MAKES 10 TO 12

ORANGE CREAM BISCUITS

*These are designed for the Strawberry Shortcake on
page 62 but, in truth, they are irresistible just spread
with butter and orange marmalade.*

> 2 cups all-purpose flour
> 1 tablespoon baking powder
> 1 tablespoon sugar
> ½ teaspoon salt
> 1¼ cups heavy cream
> 1 tablespoon grated orange zest
> 4 tablespoons butter, melted
> cinnamon sugar for sprinkling (optional
>   but delicious for shortcakes)

Preheat oven to 425 degrees F.

Combine flour, baking powder, sugar, and salt in
large mixing bowl. Mix with fork. Gradually pour in

about 1 cup of the cream, stirring constantly with wooden spoon to evenly moisten. Add orange zest and drizzle in remaining cream, turning dough by hand until just moist enough to hold together.

Turn out onto floured board and knead about a minute. Pat dough into circle and then lightly roll to about ½-inch thickness. Cut out with 3-inch round fluted cutter or glass dipped in flour. Gather dough scraps and re-roll, being careful to handle lightly. Transfer to uncoated baking sheet, brush tops with butter and sprinkle with cinnamon sugar, if desired. Bake about 15 minutes, until lightly browned on edges. Cool on racks.

MAKES 10

CRUMPETS

You are in for a treat if you have never tasted freshly griddled crumpets. The forerunner of our English muffins and de rigueur for fireside teas, they put the flimsy store-bought type to shame. Round cookie cutters or rings are necessary to make these.

1 package dry yeast
1 teaspoon sugar
⅓ cup warm water
1¾ cups milk
2¼ cups bread flour
1 teaspoon salt
½ teaspoon baking soda

In mixing bowl, sprinkle yeast and sugar over warm water. Let stand 5 minutes.

Stir in milk, flour, salt, and soda. Cover with plastic wrap and let stand for 30 minutes.

Grease several 3-inch cookie cutters. Arrange on greased griddle, over medium heat. Spoon scant

3 tablespoons batter into each ring. Reduce heat and cook about 10 minutes or until tops are full of holes and batter is set. Remove rings. If desired, turn crumpets and cook until browned on other side. Or, remove from griddle and toast in toaster, or fireplace.

MAKES 16

Blends

Most teas today are blends rather than the product of a single growth. Blends are either all black or all green and they include teas like Darjeeling, as well as the typical English and Irish breakfast blends and Lipton's. When tea mania was at its peak in the 18th century, most tea was blended at home.

SALLY LUNN BUNS

Lunn buns are a light egg bread, similar to brioche, brought to England by an enterprising French Huguenot woman in 1680. The traditional toppings are butter, clotted cream, and jam.

½ stick butter
1 teaspoon sugar
1 cup milk
1½ tablespoons dry yeast
3 eggs
2½ to 3 cups all-purpose flour
1 teaspoon salt
1 tablespoon milk

Grease baking sheet and two (1½-inch-wide, 18-inch-long) strips of foil.

Combine butter, sugar, and milk in saucepan and heat until milk is warm, about 110 degrees F.

(Butter does not need to melt completely.) Add yeast, blending well. Lightly beat 2 of the eggs and add to mixture.

Sift 2½ cups flour with salt into large bowl. Make a well in center and add liquid mixture. Mix well, adding flour if needed, to form soft dough. Lightly knead 2 minutes on floured board.

Cut dough in half. Shape each into a 6-inch round. Place on prepared baking sheet and secure each around its base with foil strip. Cover with clean towel and set in warm place to rise until doubled, about 1 hour.

Preheat oven to 425 degrees F.

Bake buns 20 minutes. Meanwhile, beat remaining egg with milk for glaze. Brush on tops. Return to oven for a few minutes to dry. Cool on rack. Split buns in half and toast to serve.

SERVES 4

CINNAMON PECAN POPOVERS

These big, airy popovers are best served right out of the oven.

1 cup milk
3 eggs
3 tablespoons butter, melted
1 cup all-purpose flour
1 teaspoon cinnamon
1/4 teaspoon salt
1/2 cup finely chopped pecans

Preheat oven to 400 degrees F. Grease 8 (6-ounce) custard cups and arrange on baking sheet.

In blender, combine milk, eggs, butter, flour, cinnamon, and salt. Process 30 seconds to blend. Fill prepared custard cups 1/3 full. Sprinkle tops with pecans. Bake 30 minutes or until tops are golden brown. Serve immediately.

MAKES 8

Afternoon Tea

The practice of eating tea and small cakes in the late afternoon was started by Anna, Duchess of Bedford, in the mid-1800s. As she couldn't bear the stretch from the morning meal to dinner at 8 p.m., she began nibbling snacks with her friends around 4 p.m. Apparently, she wasn't the only one in a slump, because the afternoon snack became as important to British well-being as a good raincoat or a pair of Wellingtons.

Today, afternoon tea consists of elegant sandwiches, scones, cakes, and cookies. It is served in the late afternoon at hotels and tea houses, and is still meant as a social interlude and pick-me-up before dinner.

High Tea, served closer to 6 p.m., is the working man's tea or small supper. It consists of foods like eggs, sausage, bacon, kippers, bread and cheese, with something sweet for dessert.

Cream Tea is a light snack of scones, served with clotted Devonshire cream and jam rather than butter.

Fireside Tea is served at the hearth where guests toast bread, crumpets, and muffins over the flames, while sipping tea.

CHOCOLATE TEA BREAD

This fine-textured, dark quick bread is sublime spread with a thin layer of Vanilla Cream Cheese (page 93).

> 1¾ cups all-purpose flour
> 1 tablespoon baking powder
> 1 teaspoon baking soda
> 6 tablespoons butter, softened
> ¾ cup plus 2 tablespoons sugar
> 2 eggs
> 2 teaspoons vanilla
> ½ cup Dutch process cocoa
> 1 cup buttermilk
> ¾ cup walnuts, roughly chopped

Preheat oven to 350 degrees F. Lightly grease 9 x 5 x 3-inch loaf pan.

Combine flour, baking powder, and soda in bowl. Mix with fork.

In another bowl, cream butter and sugar together with electric mixer. Add eggs and vanilla and lightly beat until smooth. Sprinkle in cocoa and beat until smooth; then pour in buttermilk and mix. Add flour mixture and lightly beat just until flour disappears. Lightly beat in nuts, and spoon batter into prepared pan. Smooth top and bake 1 hour, until tester inserted in center comes out clean. (Do not fret about a cracked top.) Let cool in pan on rack, then invert to remove and cool on rack.

MAKES 1 LOAF

The Birth of the Bush

Legend has it that Bodhidharma, the Indian monk who introduced Zen to China, fell asleep while meditating for many seasons before the same wall. Angry with himself for losing concentration, he cut off his eyelids and flung them to the ground where they grew into the first tea bush.

SIMPLE CAKES AND COOKIES

QUEEN OF HEARTS

The perfect accompaniment to a fragrant cup of Earl Grey.

2 sticks butter, softened
1 cup confectioners' sugar
2 teaspoons almond extract
2¼ cups all-purpose flour
¾ cup finely ground almonds
¼ teaspoon salt
½ cup milk
½ cup seedless raspberry jam

Cream together butter and ¾ cup of the confectioners' sugar. Beat in almond extract.

In another bowl, combine flour, almonds, and salt. Add milk and then flour mixture to creamed butter in three batches, alternating milk and dry ingredients. Mix thoroughly at medium speed between additions. Knead gently on board to form a disk. Cover with plastic and chill at least 3 hours.

To bake, preheat oven to 350 degrees F. Sift remaining ¼ cup sugar into small bowl and set aside.

Cut dough in half and return one piece to refrigerator. Roll out dough on board dusted with confectioners' sugar to ⅛-inch thickness. Cut out with tiny heart-shaped cookie cutter (about 1½ inches wide) and transfer to ungreased cookie sheets. Bake until edges are golden, 18 to 20 minutes. Transfer to racks. Re-roll scraps and remaining dough and continue cutting and baking.

While still hot, spread the bottoms of half the cookies with jam. Place an uncoated cookie over the jelly, bottom-to-bottom, and press together to sandwich the filling. Let cool and then dip each in confectioners' sugar to coat, shaking off excess sugar. Cool on racks before storing.

MAKES ABOUT 40 TINY COOKIES

HAZELNUT MILANESE

*We like to keep these miniature nut cakes in ziplock bags
in the freezer for unexpected guests.*

1 cup hazelnuts or filberts
¾ cup confectioners' sugar
¼ cup brown sugar
½ cup cake flour
½ teaspoon salt
6 egg whites
1 stick butter, melted

Heat oven to 350 degrees F. Arrange nuts on
baking tray and toast until skins blister and loosen,
about 15 minutes. Set aside to cool and turn oven
up to 425 degrees F.

To skin nuts, rub handfuls between palms, shaking off papery skins. (They won't all come off, so
don't be too finicky.) Transfer nuts to food processor

fitted with metal blade and process until finely ground. Add the sugars, salt, and flour. Pulse until well blended and transfer to mixing bowl.

Pour the unbeaten egg whites into the nut mixture and stir to combine. Pour in the butter and stir well.

Generously grease mini muffin pan. Ladle the batter into cups, half full, and bake 15 minutes. Turn oven off and let sit in oven 5 minutes longer. Set pans on rack to cool 10 minutes, then invert to remove.

MAKES 24

How to Store

Like all foods, tea is vulnerable to light, heat, moisture, and time. Store in airtight containers at room temperature and discard after a year or so. One tea, the rare Chinese black Cheemun, is said to improve with age like wine.

JELLY POCKETS

This delicate pastry dough stuffed with a pocketful of colorful jam is another sure hit with the lunch box set.

> 1 cup all-purpose flour
> 3 tablespoons sugar
> ¼ teaspoon salt
> 1 teaspoon grated lemon zest
> 7 tablespoons butter, softened
> 1 egg
> ½ teaspoon vanilla
> 1 egg, beaten
> apricot or raspberry jam

Combine flour, sugar, salt, lemon zest, and butter in bowl. Mix with electric mixer at low speed until butter is evenly distributed and mixture is crumbly.

Beat egg with vanilla in small bowl. Pour into flour mixture and continue to beat at low speed until dough begins to hold a shape. Lightly knead on floured board, pat into disk, wrap with plastic and chill at least one hour.

To bake, preheat oven to 375 degrees F. Lightly grease baking sheet. Roll out dough on floured board to ¼-inch thickness. Cut out circles with 3-inch-wide glass or cookie cutter. Remove excess dough, place in bowl and chill. Brush the circles with egg and place ½ teaspoon jam in center of each. Fold to enclose and press edges with fingertips to seal. Transfer to prepared sheet and brush tops with egg. Repeat with remaining chilled dough. Bake about 15 minutes, until tops are golden and set. Transfer to racks to cool.

MAKES 16

CHOCOLATE PECAN BARS

*A layer of brownie-like crust topped with
a suave layer of chocolate.*

1 stick butter, softened
½ cup brown sugar
½ cup finely chopped pecans
1 egg
1 teaspoon rum or vanilla
1½ cups all-purpose flour
½ teaspoon salt
¼ teaspoon baking soda
½ teaspoon cinnamon
6 ounces heavy cream
6 ounces semisweet chocolate, chopped
16 pecan halves

Preheat oven to 350 degrees F.

Combine butter, brown sugar, chopped pecans, egg, and rum or vanilla in mixing bowl and beat with electric mixer until smooth. In another bowl, combine flour, salt, baking soda, and cinnamon and add to butter mixture. Beat until smooth ball forms. Lightly knead and then press in even layer in 9-inch square baking pan. Bake 15 minutes. Cool in pan on rack 30 minutes.

Meanwhile bring cream to full boil in small saucepan. Place chopped chocolate in medium bowl. Pour hot cream, all at once, into chocolate and whisk until smooth. Set aside to cool and thicken at room temperature, whisking occasionally.

When cake is cool, invert to remove and carefully place on cutting board. Spread chocolate generously over top and cut into small squares. Press a pecan half in the center of each and chill to set.

MAKES 16

MOM'S APPLE CAKE

Helene's mother, Ida, is responsible for this wholesome brown cinnamon cake that cuts neatly into squares. Don't be concerned with the stiffness of the batter. Water released as the apples cook make the cake exceptionally moist.

2 cups all-purpose flour
1 tablespoon baking powder
2 teaspoons cinnamon
2 sticks butter, softened
1½ cups sugar
3 eggs
2 teaspoons vanilla
¾ cup roughly chopped walnuts
3 medium apples, peeled, cored, and thinly sliced

Preheat oven to 350 degrees F. Grease 9 x 13-inch baking pan.

Sift together flour, baking powder, and cinnamon and set aside.

In mixing bowl with electric mixer, beat the butter until smooth and creamy. With mixer on medium, drizzle in sugar. Add eggs, one at a time, beating well after each addition. Add dry ingredients and mix until batter is smooth. Slowly beat in walnuts and apples just to combine. Spoon batter (it will be thick) into pan and smooth top with spatula. Bake 50 to 60 minutes until top is brown and sides pull away from pan. Let cool in pan 10 minutes and cut into squares to serve. Apple cake is delicious served warm with whipped cream, vanilla ice cream, or just a sprinkling of confectioners' sugar.

MAKES 8 LARGE SQUARES OR 16 MINIATURES

GINGERBREAD CAKE

Gingerbread, the traditional English spice cake,
is great for freezing.

6 tablespoons butter, softened
1 cup brown sugar
½ cup molasses
1 tablespoon grated orange zest
1 teaspoon grated lemon zest
2 eggs
2½ cups all-purpose flour
2 teaspoons baking soda
1 tablespoon plus 1 teaspoon ground ginger
1 teaspoon cinnamon
½ teaspoon nutmeg
½ teaspoon salt
½ cup buttermilk
½ cup fresh orange juice
½ cup sugar

Preheat oven to 350 degrees F.
Beat butter at low speed, then add sugar and beat at low speed until smooth. Beat in molasses and zests. Add eggs, one at a time, beating thoroughly and scraping down bowl between additions.

In another bowl, mix together flour, baking soda, ginger, cinnamon, nutmeg, and salt. Combine buttermilk and ¼ cup of orange juice.

Add dry ingredients and buttermilk mixture to creamed mixture in thirds, beating between additions and ending with liquid. Pour into 9-inch square greased cake pan and bake 45 minutes, until tester inserted in center comes out clean. Cool in pan on rack 10 minutes. Turn out onto rack to cool.

Make glaze by combining in small saucepan ¼ cup orange juice and sugar. Bring to boil and cook until liquid is clear and syrup is formed. Pierce cake all over with toothpick and generously brush hot glaze over top. Cut into squares to serve.

MAKES 16 SQUARES

CITRUS POUND CAKE

We have never been able to turn down a golden slice of excellent pound cake.

4 eggs
1 ¼ cups sugar
½ teaspoon salt
¾ cup half-and-half
2 teaspoons each finely grated lemon
   and orange zest
1 ¾ cups all-purpose flour
1 ¼ teaspoons baking powder
1 stick butter, melted and cooled
¼ cup orange juice

Preheat oven to 325 degrees F. Line 9 x 5 x 3-inch loaf pan with greased waxed paper.

Lightly beat eggs with electric mixer. Slowly add sugar and salt and beat until fluffy. Beat in half-and-half and zests.

Sift flour with baking powder. Add to egg mixture and beat until smooth. Stir in butter. Pour into prepared pan and bake about 1¼ hours, or until cake tester comes out clean. Cool in pan on wire rack. Pierce top all over with toothpick and brush with orange juice. Cool completely, then invert to remove.

SERVES 10 TO 12

Tea in India

Although it grew there in the wild, the British introduced tea to India as a cash crop in an effort to end the Chinese tea monopoly during the 19th century. They succeeded by cultivating the fields in Assam and Darjeeling that were to become the world's most productive black tea gardens. Today India is the world's largest producer of tea and its leaves are traded on the world market at auction houses in London and Calcutta. The Indian preference is for chai or black tea boiled with condensed milk, sugar, and spices (see page 85).

DUNDEE CAKE

This traditional dense, dry aromatic loaf seems made just for a fragrant tea or brandy.

1 ¼ cups all-purpose flour
½ teaspoon baking powder
¼ teaspoon salt
½ cup golden raisins
½ cup currants
¼ cup candied citron
¼ cup slivered almonds
1 stick butter, softened
⅓ cup sugar
2 eggs, beaten
2 tablespoons brandy
candied cherries and whole blanched
    almonds (optional)

Preheat oven to 250 degrees F. Line 9 x 5 x 3-inch loaf pan with buttered waxed paper.

Sift flour with baking powder and salt. Add fruits and nuts and toss to coat.

In bowl, cream butter and sugar until light. Slowly beat in eggs, then brandy. Add flour mixture and beat until combined. Place batter in prepared pan. Decorate top, if desired, with cherries and almonds. Bake 1½ hours, or until firm to touch. Cool 10 minutes on wire rack then remove from pan and cool completely.

SERVES 12

Tea and the Caffeine Menace

Black tea has about half the caffeine of coffee, while milder green and Oolongs have even less. Nonetheless, manufacturers are rushing decaffeinated teas to market to placate the caffeine police.

TARTS
PUDDINGS
AND
ICE CREAMS

COCONUT LEMON CURD TARTLETS

Do not attempt to bake this crumbly, dry crust in a larger pan. It is designed to serve as a bite-sized platform for a dab of rich, smooth lemon curd and a tart berry.

CRUST
1½ cups all-purpose flour
2 tablespoons sugar
½ cup unsweetened grated coconut
¼ teaspoon salt
1 stick butter, room temperature
Lemon Curd (page 88)
raspberries for garnish (optional)

Preheat oven to 350 degrees F.

In large bowl, combine flour, sugar, coconut, and salt. Mix with fork. Cut butter into ¼-inch slices and add to flour. Blend with fingertips or pastry blender until medium pieces of butter are visible and dough holds a shape when pressed. Press into cups of uncoated candy tray or half the depth of mini muffin pans to form miniature pastry shells. Place on baking tray and bake until golden and dry, about 25 minutes. Cool on rack.

Remove pastries with tip of paring knife and place on plate. Top each with about a teaspoon of cold lemon curd and a raspberry. Refrigerate until serving time.

MAKES 60 MINIATURES

Herbal Teas

Drinks made from herbs or other plants are not technically teas, but rather tisanes or infusions. Make your own by steeping 1 teaspoon dried herb per cup for 5 minutes or simmering whole fresh herbs or edible flowers (like chamomile) 3 to 5 minutes before straining. Most herbs are naturally caffeine free—except South American mate which has as much caffeine as coffee.

STRAWBERRY SHORTCAKES

Our favorite all-American summer dessert is a good choice for a formal sit-down tea. All the parts can be prepared in advance and assembled as guests are seated.

8 Orange Cream Biscuits (page 30)
1½ pints strawberries, hulled and sliced
1½ tablespoons sugar
1 cup heavy cream, cold
3 tablespoons confectioners' sugar
2 teaspoons vanilla or Grand Marnier

Combine strawberries and sugar in bowl and let sit at least 1 hour at room temperature or up to 7 hours in the refrigerator. A syrup will form in the bottom of the bowl.

Pour cream into chilled mixing bowl and whisk with balloon whisk, at low speed, until cream starts to thicken. Turn speed to high, drizzle in sugar and vanilla or liqueur and whisk until soft peaks form.

To serve: slice each biscuit in half and place the bottoms on serving plates. Top each with a generous spoonful of strawberries and spoon the syrup evenly over all. Spoon the whipped cream over the berries to taste and then cover with the top piece of biscuit. To have berries and cream spilling out of the biscuit is desirable. Serve immediately.

MAKES 8

Additions to Tea

Milk, lemon, or sugar need only be added to the brisk fermented black teas that most resemble coffee-like breakfast blends and Darjeeling. No additions are necessary to fragrant greens or Oolong. Strongly flavored honey can dramatically change the flavor of tea, and purists consider even sugar a blasphemy.

The quaint custom of pouring milk into tea cups first, before the hot liquid, grew out of the need to prevent fragile porcelain tea cups from cracking. Though no longer necessary, it remains an important gesture among anglophiles.

RASPBERRY CUSTARD TART

This delicate fruit tart is simplicity itself.

CRUST

1 cup all-purpose flour
¼ teaspoon salt
2 tablespoons sugar
1 stick butter, cold and sliced in tablespoons
1 egg yolk
1 tablespoon cold water
½ teaspoon vanilla

FILLING

3 egg yolks
¼ cup sugar
¾ cup heavy cream
½ teaspoon Kirsch or vanilla
2 cups raspberries, blackberries, or blueberries
confectioners' sugar (optional)

Place flour, salt, sugar, and butter in food processor and pulse until butter is broken into small pieces. Beat egg yolk, water, and vanilla together. With machine on, pour egg through feed tube and process until dough forms ball.

Press into a disk and roll out to form an 11-inch circle. Line 10-inch tart pan with removable bottom, crimping the sides. Chill 30 minutes.

Preheat oven to 375 degrees F. Line shell with parchment or foil and fill with weights. Bake 30 minutes, until golden. Remove paper and cool.

Whisk together egg yolks and sugar until smooth. Whisk in cream and Kirsch or vanilla and pour into cooled tart shell. Sprinkle berries over the custard and bake about 30 minutes until set but not browned. Cool in pan on rack and dust with confectioners' sugar, if desired.

SERVES 8 TO 10

TRIPLE JAM TART

*Select jams with an eye towards flavor and color contrast
in this colorful showcase tart.*

1½ cups all-purpose flour
½ teaspoon salt
½ cup shortening
2 to 3 tablespoons ice water
Raspberry, apricot, and boysenberry jams,
  or other jams as desired

In bowl, combine flour and salt. With pastry
blender or two knives, cut in shortening until
mixture is crumbly. Gradually sprinkle water over
mixture, blending well with fork. On lightly floured
surface, roll three quarters of the dough out to
11-inch circle. Press into 9-inch tart pan with
removable bottom and trim edge.

Preheat oven to
375 degrees F.

Roll remaining dough
and scraps between palms
to form two ¼-inch thick,
12-inch long ropes and
two 24-inch long ropes.

Twist 12-inch ropes together to
form braid. Form 4-inch circle and place in center of
dough in pan, pressing lightly to seal. Twist 24-inch
ropes together to form 8-inch circle. Press between
center circle and edge. The tart should now be parti-
tioned in three sections. Chill 15 minutes.

Fill each sections with a scant ¼-inch layer of a
different jam. Bake 40 minutes, or until crust is
golden. Cool on rack.

SERVES 12

SOUR CHERRY TRIFLE CUPS

Here is an easy version of the classic British tipsy pudding.

> ½ cup dried sour cherries
> 2 tablespoons brandy
> ¼ cup cream sherry
> 1 (10.75-ounce) pound cake, cut into
>   1-inch cubes
> 2 cups prepared custard or vanilla pudding
> ½ cup heavy cream, whipped
> sliced almonds, toasted for garnish

Combine cherries, brandy, and sherry in small saucepan. Place over low heat until almost simmering. Remove from heat and let stand 30 minutes.

Place layer of cake cubes in bottom of each of 4 wine goblets or dessert dishes. Top with a third of cherries with liquid, then custard. Repeat layers twice,using remaining cake cubes, cherries and custard. Cover with whipped cream and sprinkle with almonds. Chill at least 2 hours.

SERVES 4

Tea in Japan

Tea migrated to Japan from China in the 9th century. Green tea remains the hot beverage of choice in Japan, with people sipping everyday green tea, or bancha steeped from leaves, most of the time, while saving matcha, or powdered green tea, for the tea ceremony. Green tea is considered one of the reasons the Japanese have a low rate of stomach cancer.

The Japanese tea ceremony elevates the act of sharing food and drink to ritual. In a precise service practiced by students and master, attention is focused on the simple acts of pouring tea, offering the cup, and the placement of utensils and flowers. In the words of Okakura, "It is the tender attempt to accomplish something possible in this impossible thing we know as life."

GINGER-ORANGE MARMALADE ICE CREAM

3 cups heavy cream
1 cup milk
½ cup slivered fresh ginger
1 (16-ounce) jar orange marmalade
4 egg yolks

In saucepan, combine cream, milk, and ginger. Bring to boil, reduce heat and simmer 30 minutes. Pour through sieve, pressing ginger with back of spoon to extract as much flavor as possible. Discard ginger. Return strained liquid to pan and stir in marmalade. Bring to gentle boil, stirring to melt marmalade.

In bowl, beat yolks until slightly thickened. Slowly whisk in about 1 cup hot cream mixture, then pour all into pan and cook over low heat, stirring constantly, until thick enough to coat spoon. Cool slightly, then cover with plastic wrap and chill at least 4 hours.

Freeze in ice cream maker according to manufacturer's instructions. Transfer to freezer container, cover tightly, and freeze ½ to 2 hours before serving.

MAKES ABOUT 5 CUPS

How to Brew Tea

To brew loose tea, bring cold water to a boil in kettle. Place 1 teaspoon tea leaves per cup in infuser or directly into pot and add hot water. Let steep about 4 minutes and strain leaves or remove infuser to serve. Always serve tea piping hot and refresh with more hot water as needed.

ROSEMARY-ORANGE SORBET

Here is a thoroughly civilized dessert for an August afternoon tea or dinner party.

1 cup sugar
1 tablespoon grated orange zest
1 cup water
1 tablespoon crushed fresh rosemary leaves
2 cups orange juice
2 tablespoons lemon juice
rosemary sprigs
1 egg white, beaten until frothy
sugar for coating

In saucepan, mix sugar, orange zest, and water. Bring to boil, stirring occasionally. When liquid is clear, remove from heat and stir in rosemary. Let stand 10 minutes. Strain, discarding rosemary and zest. Stir in orange and lemon juices. Freeze in ice cream maker according to manufacturer's directions. Serve garnished with rosemary sprigs dipped in egg white, then in sugar.

SERVES 6 TO 8

Tea in Russia

Tea traveled from China to Russia, via Mongolia and Siberia, in the 17th century, but it didn't really catch on until the French declared it fashionable in the 19th century. The samovar, a large urn for brewing and serving hot tea continuously, lemon slices, the practice of sweetening tea with a lump of sugar, and smoky Russian Caravan tea (redolent of camels trekking too close to campfires!) are Russia's contribution to tea culture.

LEMON AND HONEY SYLLABUB

*This thin custard was traditionally served as a beverage,
though we consider it a dessert.*

½ cup almond macaroon crumbs
⅓ cup Madeira
juice and grated zest of 1 lemon
½ cup honey
1½ cups heavy cream
additional macaroon crumbs for garnish

Place cookie crumbs in bowl and sprinkle with 2 tablespoons Madeira. Set aside.

In separate bowl, beat lemon juice and peel with honey and remaining Madeira. Add cream and beat until thick. Gently stir in macaroons. Spoon mixture into wine glasses or dessert cups. Garnish with macaroon crumbs and serve with spoon.

SERVES 6

LEMON-HERB TEA SHERBET

2½ cups water
6 lemon herb tea bags
½ cup sugar
¼ cup light corn syrup

Bring 1½ cups water to boil. Add tea bags and steep 5 minutes. Remove bags and press out as much liquid as possible. Add remaining water, sugar, and corn syrup. Bring to simmer, stirring to dissolve sugar. Simmer 2 minutes.

Cool, then chill. Freeze in ice cream maker according to manufacturer's instructions.

SERVES 4

ICED TEAS
AND
HOT TONICS

CRANBERRY ORANGE SPICE COOLER

This is fresher and less sweet than the commercial drinks.

4 bags orange spice tea
2 cups water
2 tablespoons sugar
⅓ cup dried cranberries
4 strips orange zest
juice of 1 orange
cold sparkling water

Combine tea bags and water in saucepan. Boil down to about 1½ cups. Discard tea bags. Stir in sugar. Add cranberries and orange zest. Chill.

To serve, pour into 4 tall iced glasses. Add orange zest and cranberries. Top with sparkling water.

SERVES 4

HERBAL TEA SMOOTHIE

1 cup boiling water
3 bags almond herbal tea
2 tablespoons sugar
1 medium banana
1 cup sliced ripe fresh fruit, such as strawberries,
    peaches, apricots, plums, or pineapple
1 cup vanilla ice cream
5 ice cubes

In teapot, pour water over tea bags, cover and brew 5 minutes. Remove bags and stir in sugar. Chill.

In blender, combine tea, banana, fruit, and ice cream. Process until blended. With blender running, add ice cubes, one at a time, until blended.

SERVES 2 TO 3

ICED GINGER LEMONGRASS TEA

1 quart water
¾ cup sliced lemongrass
4 (¼-inch) slices fresh ginger
¼ cup brown sugar
1 lemon, thinly sliced

Combine water, lemongrass, ginger, and brown sugar in saucepan. Bring to boil, reduce to simmer and cook 5 minutes. Strain into pitcher, add lemon slices and chill. Serve in tall iced glasses.

SERVES 4

Tea on the Rocks

Iced tea, the tea that Americans prefer, was introduced by an Englishman at Chicago's Columbia Exposition in the summer of 1893. In an attempt to get sweltering fair-goers to drink tea, he poured it over ice and a national predilection was born. Today bottled iced tea is the fastest growing section at the supermarket.

TEA SANGRIA PUNCH

Brilliant, flavorful hibiscus adds another citrus note to the classic fruited wine drink. Highlight the colors by serving in a glass pitcher.

2 cups boiling water
8 bags hibiscus tea
½ cup sugar
1 orange, cut in eighths
1 lemon, cut in eighths
2 limes, cut in eighths
1 (750-ml) bottle dry red wine
¼ cup brandy

Pour water over tea bags in teapot. Cover and steep 5 minutes. Stir in sugar until dissolved. Set aside to cool. Squeeze juice from fruit into large pitcher, dropping squeezed fruit in as you go. Add wine, brandy and tea. Chill. Serve over ice.

SERVES 8 TO 10

HOT CHRISTMAS TEA

1 ⅓ cups water
6 bags black tea
1 cinnamon stick, broken
3 whole cloves
⅓ cup sugar
1 ⅓ cups cranberry juice cocktail
1 cup Burgundy wine
orange, pear, or apple slices studded with
    cloves as garnish

In saucepan, bring water to boil. Add tea and spices, cover and let stand 5 minutes. Remove tea bags. Stir in sugar, cranberry juice, and wine. Return to medium heat and stir until sugar is dissolved and mixture is heated through.

Serve in cups with fruit slices as garnish.

SERVES ABOUT 8

THE UNCAPPUCCINO

This is for the tea drinkers who feel neglected living in a cappuccino and latte world.

2 cups boiling water
4 bags cinnamon tea
½ cup warm milk
2 tablespoons brown sugar
whipped cream and cinnamon for
 sprinkling

In teapot, pour water over tea bags. Cover and brew 5 minutes. Remove and discard tea bags. Stir in milk and sugar. Pour into cups and top with whipped cream. Sprinkle with cinnamon.

SERVES 4

FRESH MINT TEA

Any fresh herb or plant can be boiled and steeped for homemade tea: thyme, rosemary, and, of course, chamomile are some of our favorites. The flavors are much clearer than processed teas.

1 quart water
½ bunch fresh mint
honey

Bring water to boil in saucepan. Stir in mint and simmer 3 minutes. Strain into teapot or cups and serve with honey.

SERVES 4

INDIAN SPICED TEA

1 cup water
1 cup half-and-half
2 tablespoons loose black tea, such as Ceylon
1 cinnamon stick
1 slice fresh ginger
3 cloves
2 teaspoons sugar

Bring water and half-and-half to boil in small saucepan. Add remaining ingredients, stir and reduce to simmer. Cook 10 minutes. Strain and serve hot or chill and serve over ice.

SERVES 2

EASY
SPREADS

LEMON CURD

Lemon curd is a sweet-tart custard traditionally spread on plain scones and muffins. It is also one of our favorite summer pie fillings.

3 eggs
¾ cup sugar
1 tablespoon grated lemon zest
1 cup fresh lemon juice
4 tablespoons butter, cold, cut in 4 pieces

In bowl or top of double boiler, whisk eggs until smooth. Whisk in sugar, zest, and lemon juice. Place over small pan of simmering water and cook over low heat, stirring constantly with wooden spoon until thick and pale yellow, 7 to 10 minutes. Stir in butter, one tablespoon at a time, until thoroughly combined and smooth. Set bowl over ice, stirring occasionally, to cool. Cover with plastic wrap touching surface and store in refrigerator up to 5 days.

MAKES 1½ CUPS

RHUBARB RASPBERRY JAM

Good news! Sterilization is not necessary if jam is stored covered in the refrigerator and used within four weeks.

4 cups 1-inch rhubarb pieces
½ cup water
4 cups raspberries
5 cups sugar

Sterilize 6 (8-ounce) jars and lids. In large pot, combine rhubarb and water. Simmer until fruit is soft. Add berries and simmer until soft. Stir in sugar and bring to boil, stirring. Boil until mixture registers 221 to 224 degrees F. on candy thermometer. Skim off foam. Pour into prepared jars, filling within ⅛-inch of tops. Wipe rims clean and seal.

MAKES 6 (8-OUNCE) JARS

CLOTTED CREAM

Thick, rich luxurious cream is perfect for dabbing on crumbly scones.

■ 2 cups heavy cream

Cook cream in top of double boiler over simmering water until reduced by about half. It should be the consistency of butter, with a golden "crust" on the top.

Transfer, including crust, to bowl. Cover and let stand 2 hours, then refrigerate at least 12 hours. Stir crust into cream before serving. Serve on Sally Lunn Buns (page 34), English muffins, or scones.

MAKES ABOUT 1 CUP

HONEY THYME BUTTER

*Beware of bees when serving this fragrant topping
in the summer garden.*

1 stick butter, softened
2 tablespoons orange blossom honey
1 teaspoon chopped fresh thyme

Combine butter, honey, and thyme in food processor or blender. Process until blended. Serve as spread on toast, muffins, biscuits, or scones.

MAKES ABOUT 1 CUP

CHUTNEY CREAM CHEESE

1 (8-ounce) package cream cheese, softened
¼ cup chopped mango chutney
1 teaspoon curry powder (optional)

In food processor or blender, combine cheese, chutney, and curry powder. Process until well blended. Use as spread on toast, muffins, scones, biscuits, or crackers.

MAKES 1 CUP

VANILLA CREAM CHEESE

*This sweetened spread is designed to complement the
Chocolate Tea Bread on page 38.*

1 (3-ounce) package cream cheese, softened
1 teaspoon vanilla
2 tablespoons confectioners' sugar

Beat ingredients together just
to combine and transfer to
serving crock.

MAKES ½ CUP

GINGER-LIME MARMALADE

*Here is a strong flavored marmalade for rough-hewn
plain breads and crumpets.*

> 5 limes
> 1 lemon
> 2 cups water
> Sugar
> 1/3 cup slivered crystallized ginger

Peel limes and lemon trimming away white part.
Cut skin in fine 3/4-inch long slivers. Discard pith
and seeds and finely chop fruit, reserving juices.
Mix skin, fruit and juice in large heavy pan. Add
water and simmer, uncovered, 10 minutes. Cover
and let stand overnight.

Sterilize 4 (8-ounce) jars and lids. Measure fruit
mixture. For each cup, add 1½ cups sugar. Return to

pan, stir in ginger and bring to boil over medium-low heat, stirring to dissolve sugar. Boil slowly, stirring occasionally, until mixture registers 220 degrees F on candy thermometer, about 30 minutes. Remove from heat and stir 1 minute. Skim off foam and ladle into prepared jars, filling to within ⅛ inch of tops. Wipe rims and seal with lids. Store in a cool place.

MAKES 4 (8-OUNCE) JARS

Tea and Health

Hot tea with lemon and honey is a universal cold remedy and anyone who has ever stumbled out of bed with a queasy stomach knows that tea is much more appealing at such times than espresso. More dramatic claims regarding tea's current healing qualities include its ability to lower blood pressure and cholesterol, prevent cancer, promote healthy liver function, and reduce tooth decay.

QUICK FIG JAM

Not quite a recipe, these are notes culled from Helene's memory of a backyard with a fig tree—definitely worth a try if you have such a tree and the month is September.

ripe purple figs, skins bursting
sugar
lemon juice

Remove stems and peel figs, roughly chop. Place in saucepan with a minimum of sugar to taste and bring to boil. Reduce to simmer and cook, stirring frequently, until thickened to taste, about 15 minutes. Mash lightly with wooden spoon and season with lemon juice. Store in sealed container in the refrigerator.